T0193438

JENNIFER DUNAGAN
ILLUSTRATED BY EMMANUEL J. DUNAGAN

Santana MEETS Santa

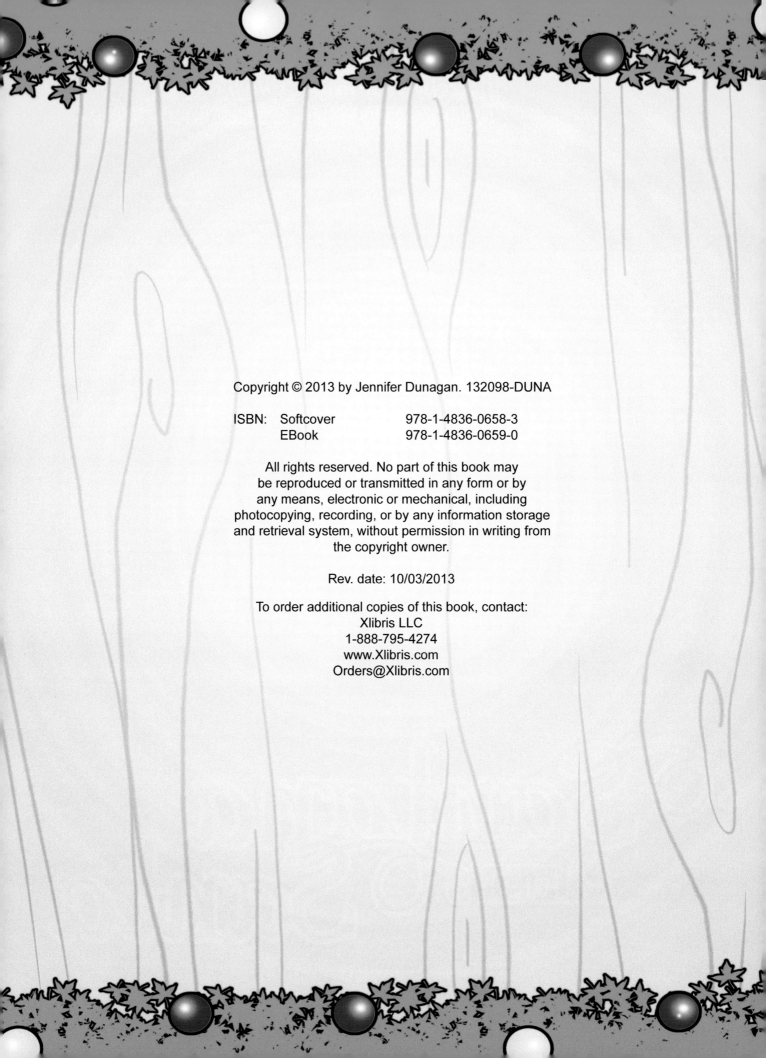

Dedication

This book is dedicated to my father and mother, Webster and Joyce Bossett. You have always been there for me and I love you for giving me so many wonderful Christmases.

In Loving Memory of Santana Bobana Dunagan,
Auntie Jennie and Uncle Curtis's angel baby dog.

SANTANA MEETS SANTA

Santana often heard about Santa Claus. During the holidays, everytime he watched television there was something on about Santa and Christmas. Auntie Jennie told him that during the month of December he would hear a lot about Christmas, the birthday of The Baby Jesus, and about Santa, his reindeer and his elves.

Santana already liked Santa because his name sounds like Santana's. He liked Santa's bright suit and long white beard. He thought it amazing that Santa brought good little children the toys they asked for. He wondered if Santa brought good puppies and kittys what they wanted too.

Uncle Curtis told Santana that even though animals couldn't talk, Santa somehow knew if they had been good and what they wanted for Christmas. Santana had to think awhile before he decided what he wanted most. He knew he had to be a good and obedient puppy. He couldn't misbehave like he did on Halloween.

It was almost Christmas Eve and he watched Auntie Jennie wrap presents for their family and friends. They were going to Houston, Texas where Auntie Jennie was born and where his brother, Bosco lived. His sister, Lucy was going with them also. He hoped Santa knew where they would be so they would still get their presents. They brought so many pretty colored packages and even packed suitcases full of dress-up clothes and some of Santana and Lucy's toys. He could hardly wait: this would be his first real Christmas.

Once he got to Houston he was anxious to see his brother, Bosco and his cousins, Jerry, Daisy and Buddy. He knew they were all going to spend the night at Nee-Nee and Granddaddy's house on Christmas Eve. "I guess Santa will know which puppy gets what toy," he wondered. Just as Santana and Lucy were about to put their toys away, Bosco burst in through the back door and jumped so high, he looked like a baby kangaroo.

Santana thought it was really fun to chase Bosco in the house, but Nee-Nee told them to go outside and play. He actually wanted to help Uncle Curtis, Granddaddy, Uncle Mark, Eric and Riley with the decorations; but he guessed only humans could do that.

It was very cold outside. Everyone had their own chore to complete. Auntie Jennie, Nee-Nee, Aunt Greta and Aunt Mary were busy cooking turkey, ham and other delicious smelling foods. Stacy, Marissa and all the cousins and grandchildren, Yaslyn, Quinn, Zach, Samantha, Jessica, Alex, Aureanna, Mason and Re`jon were wrapping and placing presents under the Christmas tree while eating Christmas cookies.

It was Christmas Eve and Santana knew Santa was coming. It was beginning to get dark and it was almost time for everyone to go to sleep and wait for Santa. Santana had a secret plan that no one else knew anything about.

Granddaddy turned on the tree lights and all the outside lights. "Wow", Santana thought; "that's the most beautiful thing I've ever seen!" There was a Nativity scene, lots of brightly lit deer and red, green and white lights everywhere. All the dogs ran outside and sat in the grass for a long time watching the lights go on and off.

When it started to get really cold, Auntie Jennie went outside to get them so that they could have a treat and go to bed. They were all going to sleep in the laundry room where it was nice and warm. It felt good to be with his family.

After everyone went to bed and all the other dogs were still asleep, Santana thought he heard a noise. He got up and tip toed into the living room where all the little kids left cookies and milk for Santa. Santana's secret was to surprise Santa and share cookies and milk with him. Santa gave him doggie treats instead and let him sit on his lap.

Santana knew Santa was really special because he understood everything Santana was thinking. Santa told him to always obey grown-ups and to do the right thing. Santa placed a special little drum around Santana's neck and told him to wake everyone up in the morning by beating the drum. Santa even called him 'The Little Drummer Dog." Santana was so excited.

He was getting very sleepy, so Santa told him to go back to bed because he had to deliver lots more presents to others that night.

Santana woke everyone up and they were surprised to see the drum that Santa had given him. Everyone hurried downstairs to open presents.

Afterwards, the whole family went to church. The children pretended to have church services for the dogs. They even dressed them in their new Christmas sweaters.

For dinner, there was an adult table, a kids table and a doggie table. The doggies had turkey flavored bones with gravy, potatoe pie flavored treats and egg nog flavored water.

After dinner the kids went outside to play with the dogs and their toys. They also brought homemade cookies to the neighbors,the Spencers, the Herringtons and the Hernandez family. They visited Zach's friend, Janie and her Chihuahuas, Buttons and Bows. Lucy was so excited that she wiggled out of her leash and scratched on Janie's door so that she could play with Buttons and Bows.

Santana had never been so happy. It was a magical holiday. He hoped all of his Christmases would be this special. He loved Auntie Jennie and Uncle Curtis very much and was happy to have such a wonderful, loving family to share Christmas with.

Printed in the United States
by Baker & Taylor Publisher Services